To every reader, in the hope that you will feed the resistance

– M.P.

To my Me-Me, who passed down her love of cooking and community to my mom and me

– A.H.

MAGIC CAT PUBLISHING

Recipes for Change © 2023 Lucky Cat Publishing Ltd
Text © 2023 Michael Platt
Illustrations © 2023 Alleanna Harris
First Published in 2023 by Magic Cat Publishing, an imprint of Lucky Cat Publishing Ltd, Unit 2 Empress Works, 24 Grove Passage, London E2 9FQ, UK

A catalogue record for this book is available from the British Library.

ISBN 978-1-913520-55-7

The illustrations were created digitally
Set in Patrick Hand, Print Bold and The Rouged

Published by Rachel Williams and Jenny Broom
Designed by Stephanie Jones and Ella Tomkins
Edited by Helen Brown

Manufactured in Malaysia

1 3 5 7 9 8 6 4 2

FSC www.fsc.org MIX Paper from responsible sources FSC® C017888

Recipes FOR CHANGE

Written by
Michael Platt

Illustrated by
Alleanna Harris

MAGIC CAT PUBLISHING

Contents

Safety Note: Cooking is great fun, but frying, sharp knives, ovens, and other elements of cooking can be dangerous. Always have an adult around you while you cook, to supervise and assist as needed.

Dear Reader,

I have a strong pride and appreciation for my culture. Resilient, courageous and diverse, Black leaders and changemakers of the past and present inspire me every day, and with every challenge we have overcome, something has sustained us:

Food.

Food plays – and has played – a vital role in strengthening and shaping Black empowerment. For centuries, we have used food to feed our families, friends and communities; to celebrate our achievements; and to remember and respect how far we've come. From civil rights activism of the past to the Black Lives Matter movement of today, food continues to empower us.

In this book, I retell the stories of twelve momentous months in Black history to honour the relationship that food and protests have always had, and then share one of my own recipes inspired by these events. I hope this book encourages you to tell your story, share your recipes and feel empowered, too.

Michael Platt

Food justice advocate and baker

January

It was a cold January morning in Oakland, California, when Huey and Bobby first opened a church's doors to provide a free breakfast to school children.

Three years earlier, they had founded the Black Panther Party, a movement to empower Black people across America who were suffering from inequality. The Black Panthers knew that food affects a child's education, and so every morning they served milk, toast, eggs, bacon and creamy grits to the young people who needed it most.

The Free Breakfast for School Children Program was set up because hunger made it difficult for many Black children from poor communities to learn in school.

The Black Panthers introduced the scheme in other cities. By the end of the first year, they had served breakfast to 20,000 children across the country.

Huey P. Newton and Bobby Seale
Year: 1969

The Black Panther Party's creamy grits

Serves 4

- 110g grits, fine cornmeal, maize meal or instant polenta
- 700ml milk
- salt, for seasoning
- 15g butter, softened
- 55g light brown sugar
- 1 tbsp double cream
- butter, for topping

- Place the grits, cornmeal, maize meal or polenta in a saucepan.
- Pour in the milk and add a pinch of salt. Cook, stirring continuously, over a medium heat for approximately 5 minutes, or until the mixture begins to thicken.
- Remove from the heat and stir in the brown sugar and cream.
- Top with butter and serve immediately.

February

On the first day in February, Ezell, Franklin, Joseph and David walked into the Woolworth store in Greensboro, North Carolina, and sat down at the 'Whites Only' lunch counter.

They ordered slices of cherry pie, but the young men were refused service as the store only served Black customers at the stand-up counter. But they did not move, sitting peacefully until closing time. They returned over the next several days with more supporters. Their quiet act of rebellion sparked sit-ins across the South that helped end racial segregation.

During this time, Black people were kept apart from white people in some places in the United States. This was especially common in the South.

Ezell Blair, Jr., Franklin McCain, Joseph McNeil and David Richmond

Year: 1960

Thanks to the Greensboro Four, the Woolworth store began serving Black people at its lunch counter in July 1960. Four years later, the Civil Rights Act of 1964 made it against the law to segregate based on skin colour.

The Greensboro Sit-In's cherry protest pie

Serves 8

- 2 ready-to-bake pie crusts
- 440g canned pitted cherries, drained
- 200g caster sugar
- finely grated zest of 2 lemons
- 3 tbsp cornflour
- ½ tsp cinnamon
- ½ tsp almond extract
- a pinch of grated nutmeg
- 1 egg, lightly beaten
- 1 tbsp sugar, for dusting

- Preheat the oven to 200°C/180°C fan/gas mark 6 and grease a 23cm-diameter pie dish. Put a baking sheet in the oven to heat up.
- Roll out two-thirds of the pastry and line the pie dish, trimming off any excess.
- Line the pastry case with baking parchment and add baking beans to weigh it down. Bake for 15 minutes, then carefully remove the paper and beans and cook the pastry for 5 more minutes, or until golden.
- Mix together the rest of the ingredients and tip them into the pie dish.
- Roll out the remaining pastry and cut into long strips. Weave the strips together over the pie to form a lattice. Press down the edges to seal and trim off any excess. Brush with the beaten egg and sprinkle with sugar.
- Bake for 40 minutes, or until crisp and golden.
- Leave to cool for 20 minutes before serving.

March

Arm in arm, Martin, John and Hosea led demonstrators on a march for fair voting rights in Selma, Alabama.

Around 600 marchers reached the edge of Selma on 7 March 1965, when they were attacked by state troopers and local police. The day became known as 'Bloody Sunday'. Two days later, on 'Turnaround Tuesday', they reached the Edmund Pettus Bridge again but turned around to await a court ruling. On 21 March, they finally crossed over the Edmund Pettus Bridge, reaching the state capital, Montgomery, three days later. The marches raised awareness of the difficulties faced by Black voters and the need for national action.

At the time, Black people were legally allowed to vote, but officials made it very difficult for them to do so.

As a result of the three marches, President Lyndon B. Johnson signed the Voting Rights Act of 1965, which made it against the law to prevent Black people from voting.

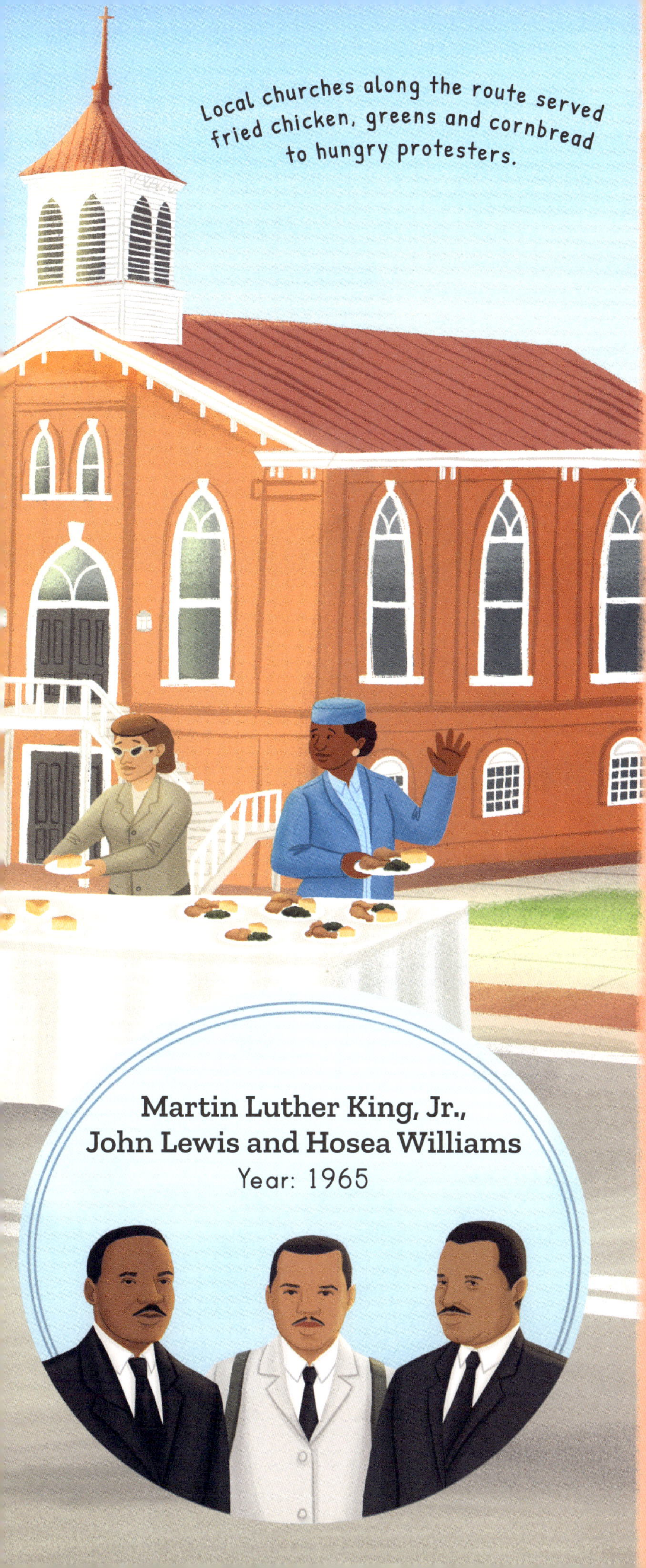

The Selma Marchers' carry-on cornbread

Serves 6

- 55g butter
- 150g fine cornmeal, maize meal or polenta
- 140g plain flour
- 1 tbsp caster sugar
- 2 tsp baking powder
- 1½ tsp salt
- 570ml buttermilk
- 2 medium eggs

- Preheat the oven to 230°C/210°C fan/ gas mark 8 and grease a 23cm-diameter cake tin.
- Place the butter in a saucepan. Cook over low heat until the butter is melted, stirring occasionally with a wooden spoon.
- Put all the dry ingredients into a large mixing bowl. Beat the buttermilk and eggs in a separate bowl, then stir in the butter.
- Add the liquid to the dry ingredients and mix together.
- Pour the batter into the cake tin and smooth down the top. Bake for 25 minutes until golden brown.
- Cool for 10 minutes, then remove from pan. Cut into wedges to serve. It's a great accompaniment to fried chicken and braised greens.

April

Throughout the seventeenth and eighteenth centuries, Black people were taken from Africa and forced into slavery in America, mainly on Southern plantations.

In the dead of night, 'conductor' Harriet led a group of runaway enslaved people from slavery in Maryland to freedom.

The route they took was called the Underground Railroad, and Harriet knew it well, having escaped slavery that way herself. It wasn't a real railroad but a series of secret safe houses called stations that hid enslaved people as they escaped to places where slavery was illegal. Harriet guided the group through the darkness, travelling through woods and foraging for food. After they ate, they followed the North Star until they found their next station: a safe place to eat and sleep when morning's light arrived.

Harriet Tubman
Years: 1850-60

The Underground Railroad's freedom fish

Serves 4

- 8 basa fillets, skin on
- salt and pepper, for seasoning
- 225g fine cornmeal, maize meal or polenta
- 1 tbsp garlic granules
- 2 tsp salt
- 1 tsp pepper
- 350ml milk
- 3 tbsp vegetable oil
- lemon wedges, for serving

- Season each fish fillet with salt and pepper to taste. Chill in the fridge for an hour.
- Mix the cornmeal, maize meal or polenta with the garlic granules, salt and pepper in a shallow bowl and set aside. Pour the milk into a second shallow bowl.
- Next, dip each fillet into the milk, then in the seasoned mix, covering it completely.
- Pour the oil into a non-stick frying pan over a medium-high heat.
- Once the pan is hot, place one fillet in the pan, skin-side down. Cook for 3 minutes, or until it is a nice golden colour. Carefully turn the fish over and cook for another 2 minutes.
- Remove the fish and let it cool slightly on a wire rack with kitchen paper underneath.
- Serve warm with a lemon wedge. Basa is a delicately flavoured fish, so it's extra tasty with hot sauce!

May

As a pot of gumbo simmered on the stove, chef Leah looked on at the students gathered in her restaurant.

They were known as Freedom Riders: Black American and white civil rights activists who rode buses together into Southern states to protest against segregated bus terminals. Leah's restaurant, Dooky Chase's, was a secret meeting place for civil rights activists when they came to New Orleans, Louisiana, and provided them with a safe place in which to plan their next protest.

Leah helped to mend the country's divisions one meal at a time. She once said, 'We changed the course of America over a bowl of gumbo.'

Leah Chase
Year: 1961

The Freedom Rides began in May 1961, and by the autumn of that same year, the government declared that segregation was not allowed in interstate terminals.

The Freedom Riders' gumbo

Serves 6

- 3 tbsp vegetable oil
- 4 andouille sausages, chopped
- 35g plain flour
- 130g tomato paste
- 3 onions, diced
- 1 carrot, diced
- 4 green peppers, diced
- 3 celery sticks, diced
- 1.4 litres chicken stock
- 30g tomato purée
- 2-3 tbsp Creole or Cajun seasoning
- 3 garlic cloves, crushed
- 6 thyme sprigs
- 1 bay leaf
- 8 okra pods, cut into 1.5cm circles
- 450g raw prawns, defrosted if frozen

- Heat the oil in a heavy-bottomed pot, add the sausages and fry for a few minutes until browned. Remove and set aside.
- Add the flour to the oil and stir continuously over a medium heat until the mixture browns.
- Turn the heat down slightly, add the tomato paste and cook for 2 minutes. Then add the onions, carrot, peppers and celery, and cook until just soft.
- Pour in the chicken stock and stir in the tomato purée, seasoning, garlic, thyme, bay leaf and browned sausage. Let it simmer gently for an hour, or until the liquid has reduced by half.
- Add the okra and prawns and simmer for 5 minutes, or until the prawns are cooked.
- Serve hot. It's delicious over buttery rice.

June

Starting in Fort Worth, Texas, eighty-nine-year-old Opal Lee began her walk to Washington, D.C. to campaign for Juneteenth to be a national holiday.

Juneteenth commemorates 19 June 1865, the day when troops came to Texas to announce the end of slavery. Although slavery should have ended more than two years earlier due to the Emancipation Proclamation, it continued in some places. Juneteenth celebrations live on, and one of the most common ways to honour the occasion is by eating red foods, from red ice lollies to red velvet cake.

'Even though there's still much work to be done, we have to celebrate the freedom that we have,' Opal said. 'That's what Juneteenth is about: celebrating freedom each step of the way.'

In June 2021, President Joe Biden officially made Juneteenth a national holiday, signing the bill into law with Opal by his side.

Juneteenth's red ice lollies

Serves 12

- 50g caster sugar
- 60ml water
- 250g strawberries
- 1 watermelon, approx. 2kg

You will also need:

- ice lolly moulds
- ice lolly sticks

- Put the sugar and water into a saucepan over a medium heat. Stir until the sugar has completely dissolved, then set the mixture aside to cool.
- Remove the strawberry leaves and purée the fruit using a hand blender or food processor. Strain the purée and set aside.
- Cut open the watermelon and scoop the flesh out into a bowl. Pick out any black seeds. Purée the flesh using a hand blender or food processor, then mix with the puréed strawberries and cooled syrup.
- Insert the sticks in the ice lolly moulds and then pour in the mixture. Freeze for around 6 hours, or until set.
- In hot weather, cool down with these refreshing lollies.

July

Standing in their kitchens in Washington, D.C., chefs Willa, Rob and Paola appealed for action.

'Calling all bakers, chefs, home bakers and cooks,' they wrote on social media. 'We are armed to fight racism with the tools we know how to utilise: our FOOD.' Naming their movement Bakers Against Racism, they organised a worldwide virtual bake sale to raise money for Black Lives Matter. Their goal was to recruit eighty bakers, but an incredible 2,000 pastry chefs and home bakers joined in to make both sweet and savoury food and raised over a million dollars!

Seven years earlier, in July 2013, the Black Lives Matter movement was founded in response to a crime watch volunteer being found not guilty in the fatal shooting of Black teenager Trayvon Martin. Then, in 2020, the death of George Floyd at the hands of a police officer placed a renewed focus on anti-Black racism.

Willa Lou Pelini, Rob Rubba and Paola Velez

Year: 2020

Black Lives Matter can refer to a hashtag, an anthem, a slogan or a social movement, all campaigning for racial justice.

The Bakers Against Racism's sweet potato hand pie

Serves 8

- 600g sweet potatoes
- 110g light brown sugar
- 1 tsp cinnamon
- 1 tsp nutmeg
- 1 tbsp double cream
- 55g butter, melted
- 500g shortcrust pastry sheets
- 710ml vegetable oil
- 25g icing sugar
- 1 tsp warm water

- Preheat the oven to 200°C/180°C fan/gas mark 6. Roast the potatoes until soft, then leave to cool.
- Scoop the potato flesh into a bowl and mix in the brown sugar, cinnamon, nutmeg, double cream and melted butter.
- Using a 12cm-diameter cutter, cut out 16 large circles from the pastry sheets. Place a tablespoon of filling on one half of each circle, fold over and use a fork to seal the edges.
- Heat the vegetable oil to 180°C in a deep-sided pan. One at a time, carefully add each pie and fry for 4 minutes or until golden brown. Alternatively, brush with melted butter and bake in the oven at 200°C/180°C fan/gas mark 6 for 15 minutes.
- While they cool, make the glaze by mixing the icing sugar with the warm water in a bowl.
- Once cooled, drizzle the pies with the glaze and serve.

August

Looking out from the Lincoln Memorial in Washington, D.C., Martin saw thousands of supporters who had gathered to hear his speech.

He started slowly, talking about what it was like to be Black in America in 1963 and the racism that still took place a hundred years after the Emancipation Proclamation. His voice then turned to hope: 'I have a dream,' he declared, 'that my four little children will one day live in a nation where they will not be judged by the colour of their skin but by the content of their character,' and he urged America to deliver on its promises of democracy.

Martin was born and raised in Atlanta, Georgia. His favourite dessert was pecan pie, which is still a staple of Southern comfort food today.

Martin Luther King, Jr.
Year: 1963

Martin gave thousands of speeches in his lifetime, and to keep going he often ate foods that nourished his soul.

Martin Luther King, Jr.'s favourite: pecan pie

Serves 8

- 250g ready-made shortcrust pastry
- 600g pecan halves
- 165g light brown sugar
- 1 tbsp plain flour
- 55g butter
- 3 medium eggs, lightly beaten
- 390g golden syrup
- 1 tsp vanilla extract
- 50ml single cream

- Preheat the oven to 220°C/200°C fan/gas mark 7 and grease a 23cm-diameter pie tin. On a lightly floured surface, roll the pastry into a circle large enough to line the pie tin. Press it into the tin, trim the edges, then chill.
- Scatter the pecans on a chopping board and chop half of them.
- Mix the sugar and flour. Warm the butter over a low heat, stirring occasionally with a wooden spoon, taking it off the heat when it is melted. Gradually stir in the sugar mixture. Beat in the eggs a little at a time, then add the golden syrup, vanilla extract, cream and the chopped pecans.
- Pour the filling mixture into the pie tin and arrange the remaining pecans on top. Bake for 5 minutes, then lower the heat to 180°C/160°C fan/gas mark 4 and bake for another 20 minutes, or until just set.
- Serve warm – it's delicious with cream or crème fraiche!

September

In Atlanta, Georgia, Robert and James looked on proudly as the kitchen door at Paschal's Restaurant swung to and fro.

Waiters brought baskets of fried chicken to tables, releasing delicious smells across the dining room. In one leather booth, Martin Luther King, Jr. huddled with a group of fellow civil rights campaigners, strategising over plates of fried chicken and mac and cheese; in another, over a peach cobbler, a group of young activists planned a protest that could change the world. The soul food diner provided a safe space for the Black community and supported those fighting for racial justice.

Robert Paschal
and James Paschal
Year: 1963

Paschal's became the unofficial headquarters of the civil rights movement, and it was one of the first restaurants to seat Black and white customers at the same table, in an era of segregated seating.

James and Robert paid money to release arrested protesters and kept the restaurant open after normal working hours to serve them free meals.

Paschal's fried chicken

Serves 4

- 1 tsp white pepper
- 1 tsp cayenne powder
- 2 tsp garlic powder
- 2 tsp smoked paprika
- 2 tsp onion powder
- 480ml buttermilk
- 1 tbsp salt
- 8 boneless and skinless chicken thighs
- 560g plain flour
- 710ml vegetable oil
- salt, for seasoning

- Mix the white pepper, cayenne powder, 1 teaspoon garlic powder, 1 teaspoon smoked paprika and 1 teaspoon onion powder in a small bowl.
- Whisk the buttermilk and salt in a bowl, then stir in the mixed seasoning. Add the chicken, then toss to coat. Transfer it all to a freezer bag and refrigerate for at least four hours, and up to overnight.
- Whisk the flour with the remaining garlic powder, paprika and onion powder. Take your chicken out of the fridge and coat it in the flour mixture.
- Heat a 10cm depth of oil in a shallow saucepan or deep-fat fryer until it reaches 175°C. Carefully lower in one chicken thigh at a time and fry undisturbed for 3 minutes. Flip the thigh, then fry for another 3 minutes until golden and crisp on both sides. Transfer to a tray lined with kitchen towel, then put the tray in a low oven to keep warm.
- Sprinkle with salt to serve.

October

A wave of quiet fell across the stadium as American sprinters Tommie and John stood on the podium at the Summer Olympics in Mexico City.

After their epic performance in the 200-metre sprint, and just before the national anthem began to play, gold-winning Tommie and bronze-winning John bowed their heads and raised black-gloved fists in the air. Their silent protest was a demand for freedom and for human rights for Black people worldwide. It became an iconic image overnight, and came to represent solidarity and strength.

The raised, clenched fist, also known as the Black Power salute, is a symbol associated with Black pride.

Tommie Smith and John Carlos

Year: 1968

Tommie and John wore black socks with no shoes to highlight Black poverty. Tommie also had a scarf around his neck for Black pride, and John wore beads to pay respect to those who died as a result of slavery.

The Black Power Salute's Olympic gold cookies

Makes up to 18

- 225g butter, softened
- 220g light brown sugar
- 200g caster sugar
- 2 medium eggs
- ½ tsp vanilla extract
- 175g plain flour
- 1 tsp bicarbonate of soda
- 1 tsp baking powder
- 75g flaxseed
- ½ tsp salt
- 270g rolled oats
- 160g dried cranberries
- 200g chopped walnuts
- 170g chocolate chips

- Preheat oven to 180°C/160°C fan/gas mark 4 and grease a flat tray.
- In a large bowl, cream together the butter, brown sugar and caster sugar until light and fluffy. Add the eggs one at a time, beating well with each addition, then stir in the vanilla.
- In a separate bowl, mix together the flour, bicarbonate of soda, baking powder, flaxseed and salt, then stir into the creamed mixture.
- Finally, stir in the oats, cranberries, walnuts and chocolate chips.
- Heap tablespoonfuls of the cookie mixture onto the greased flat tray. Wet your hands and flatten the cookies slightly.
- Bake for 15 minutes, or until golden brown.
- Allow to cool for 5 minutes, then place them on a wire rack. These cookies are a great source of energy and are delicious with milk!

November

Denison's community began preparing for Christmas on a cold November day in Greenville, North Carolina.

Due to segregation laws in the 1960s, many Greenville businesses refused to hire Black employees during the festive season. So, in response, Black people refused to purchase their gifts and food from those businesses. Boycotting these shops meant that families baked their own desserts instead, including the classic Southern banana pudding. The Black community, which made up over 30 percent of the town, also decided not to put up Christmas tree lights and decorations in their homes as a silent protest against racism.

Led by Denison, the 'Christmas Sacrifice', as it became known, was the first organised demonstration by Black people in Greenville.

The Christmas Sacrifice protest was very successful. The following year saw a large number of Black employees hired for the Christmas season.

The Christmas Sacrifice's banana pudding

Serves 8

- 70g plain flour
- a pinch of salt
- 675ml milk
- 200g caster sugar
- 4 medium egg yolks
- 55g butter
- 2 tsp vanilla extract
- 300g sponge biscuits
- 4 bananas, sliced
- 235ml double cream
- 50g icing sugar

- In a non-stick pan, whisk together the flour, salt, milk, caster sugar and egg yolks over a medium heat.
- Add in the butter and vanilla extract and whisk together.
- In a large glass bowl, place an even layer of sponge biscuits. Layer with a handful of sliced bananas, then pour a ladle of pudding on top. Repeat twice, making sure you leave a few biscuits and bananas for decorating the top!
- Whisk together the cream and icing sugar to create whipped cream. Pile the whipped cream on top, decorating with your remaining bananas and sponge biscuits.
- Refrigerate for a little over an hour.
- Serve immediately or keep in the fridge until ready to eat.

December

Georgia Gilmore

Years: 1955-56

Georgia was working as a cook in Montgomery, Alabama, on 1 December 1955 when Rosa Parks was arrested.

Rosa was coming home from work on a busy bus when a white passenger got on. According to the law at the time, Rosa had to give up her seat, but she refused and was sent to jail. Many people supported Rosa and stopped taking the bus, known as the Montgomery bus boycott. For 381 days, Georgia sold home-made pies and baked goods in support of the boycott, including her famous pound cake.

The Montgomery bus boycott brought about change. In November 1956, segregated seating laws came to an end and Black people could sit wherever they wanted on the bus.

The Montgomery Bus Boycott's pound cake

Serves 16

For the cake:

- 450g butter, softened
- 400g caster sugar
- 5 medium eggs, at room temperature, lightly beaten
- 2 tsp vanilla extract
- 90ml milk
- 280g plain flour

For the glaze:

- 65g icing sugar
- 45ml double cream
- ½ tsp vanilla extract

- Preheat the oven to 180°C/160°C fan/gas mark 4 and grease a bundt cake tin. In a large bowl, beat the butter and caster sugar with a hand mixer for 5 minutes, or until light and fluffy.
- Mix in the beaten eggs gradually, then stir in the vanilla extract and milk. Finally, sift in the flour and mix.
- Pour the mixture into the tin and spread evenly. Bake for an hour.
- Once out of the oven, leave it to cool and make the glaze. Combine the icing sugar, cream and vanilla extract.
- Transfer the cake out to a plate and drizzle the glaze over it. Slice and enjoy!

A Closer Look

Do you recognise any of the people in this book?
Learn more about them and their important work below.

Harriet Tubman
c. 1820-1913

Harriet Tubman was born into slavery on a plantation in Dorchester County, Maryland. Around her late twenties, she escaped, freeing herself before returning to liberate enslaved African Americans. Harriet sacrificed so much of her life for others; she was a spy during the Civil War, and promoted women's rights.

Robert Paschal
1909-97

Restaurateur Robert Paschal was born in Thomson, Georgia. In 1947, he relocated to Atlanta with his brother, James and set up a sandwich business. In 1959, they opened Paschal's Restaurant & Coffee Shop, which served as an unofficial headquarters for the civil rights movement and earned a reputation as Atlanta's 'Black City Hall'.

Denison Dover Garrett
1915-2011

Denison Dover Garrett was born in Pitt County, North Carolina. After his family lost their farm, they moved to Greenville, where he later became the council's first Black candidate. Denison led the county's NAACP (National Association for the Advancement of Colored People) branch and organised the 1963 Christmas Sacrifice.

Georgia Gilmore
1920-90

Georgia Gilmore was born in Montgomery, Alabama, and was working as a cook when the bus boycott began in 1955. After civil rights activist Rosa Parks was arrested for refusing to give up her seat on the bus to a white passenger, Georgia organised a group of bakers and cooks to fundraise to sustain the 381-day boycott.

James Paschal
1920-2008

Chef James Paschal was born in Thomson, Georgia, as the younger brother of Robert. In 1959, they opened Paschal's Restaurant & Coffee Shop, where their fried chicken was extremely popular. Martin Luther King, Jr. and other civil rights leaders held strategy meetings at the restaurant, and families and friends would reunite there after protests.

Leah Chase
1923-2019

Leah Chase was born in New Orleans, Louisiana, the home of Creole cooking. At 22 years old, Leah married Edgar 'Dooky' Chase II, whose parents owned the Dooky Chase Restaurant. Leah became a chef, later known as the 'Queen of Creole Cuisine', and fed the Freedom Riders, along with many other civil rights activists, including Martin Luther King, Jr.

Hosea Williams
1926-2000

Born in Attapulgus, Georgia, Hosea Williams became a civil rights activist after being attacked for drinking from a 'Whites Only' water fountain. He became one of Martin Luther King, Jr.'s most trusted advisers and played an important role in the 1965 Selma to Montgomery marches for fair voting rights.

Opal Lee
b. 1926

Born in Marshall, Texas, Opal Lee was 12 years old when, on one Juneteenth day, arsonists burned down her home in a racist attack. Opal spent the rest of her life campaigning for equality and justice, and took a symbolic walk from Fort Worth, Texas, to Washington, D.C., to gain national recognition for Juneteenth.

Martin Luther King, Jr.
1929-68

Born in Atlanta, Georgia, Martin Luther King, Jr. first experienced segregation at 6 years old, when a white friend was no longer allowed to play with him. Martin became a great believer in peaceful protest, inspired by the Indian activist Mahatma Gandhi. A year after his 'I Have a Dream' speech, Martin became the youngest man to receive the Nobel Peace Prize.

Bobby Seale
b. 1936

Born in Dallas, Texas, Bobby Seale moved to California as a young adult and met civil rights activist Huey P. Newton. They launched the Black Panther Party, which was active from 1966 to 1982. It was formed to challenge police brutality, but from 1969 onwards, its focus turned to food injustice.

John Lewis
1940-2020

John Lewis was born near Troy, Alabama, and grew up on a farm where his parents were sharecroppers (people who farm a piece of land owned by someone else). John became known for leading the 1965 Selma to Montgomery marches to protect the Black American's right to vote, and later served for 33 years in the United States House of Representatives.

David Richmond
1941-90

Born in Greensboro, North Carolina, David Richmond met Franklin McCain, Ezell Blair, Jr. and Joseph McNeil at North Carolina Agricultural and Technical State University. In 1960, they sat at a 'Whites Only' restaurant counter and returned for the next five days with more students. These protests, known as the Greensboro sit-ins, led to the desegregation of restaurants.

Franklin McCain
1941-2014

Franklin McCain was born in Union County, North Carolina. He grew up in Washington, D.C., but returned to his home state to attend North Carolina Agricultural and Technical State University. He was one of the original Greensboro Four, and once said he sees freedom as the ability to 'be oneself in society at large'.

Ezell Blair, Jr.
b. 1941

Ezell Blair, Jr. was born in Greensboro, North Carolina. His father was an NAACP member who often spoke on the subject of racial injustices. Ezell was one of the original Greensboro Four, and would later become president of his school's student government association, the campus NAACP, and the Greensboro Congress for Racial Equality.

Huey P. Newton
1942-89

Huey P. Newton was born in Monroe, Louisiana, but moved to Oakland, California, during the Second World War. He met civil rights activist Bobby Seale at college, and together they set up the Black Panther Party as a response to their strong belief that the civil rights movement had failed to improve the treatment of Black American peoples.

Joseph McNeil
b. 1942

Joseph McNeil was born in Wilmington, North Carolina, and fought against segregation in the South. He was one of the original Greensboro Four, and after staging the sit-ins, McNeil became involved with the formation of the Student Executive Committee for Justice, a student group created in response to the sit-ins.

Tommie Smith
b. 1944

Born in Clarksville, Texas, Tommie Smith earned a spot on the US National Track and Field team for the 1968 Olympics in Mexico City, where he became the first person in history to run the 200-metre race in under twenty seconds. During the medals ceremony, he and fellow athlete John Carlos each held a fist in the air as a display of solidarity for human rights for Black people.

John Carlos
b. 1945

Born in Harlem, New York, John Carlos was a gifted track-and-field athlete. Along with Tommie Smith, John earned a spot on the US National Track and Field team for the 1968 Olympics in Mexico City, and came third in the 200-metre race. Standing on the podium, Tommie and John raised their fists in a Black Power salute. They were suspended from the team and the Olympic Village for their actions.

Rob Rubba
b. 1979

Born in New Jersey, Rob Rubba was studying Fine Arts at university when he discovered his passion for pastry. He enrolled in culinary school, and was running a pop-up restaurant in Washington, D.C. when he decided to put his artistic talents to good use: creating the graphics for the Bakers Against Racism social media accounts.

Paola Velez
b. 1990

Born to parents from the Dominican Republic, chef Paola Velez was working at a doughnut pop-up in Washington, D.C., during the 2020 Black Lives Matter protests in the wake of police officer Derek Chauvin killing George Floyd. Paola conceptualised and organised Bakers Against Racism, a global virtual bake sale which raised over a million dollars.

Willa Lou Pelini
b. 1994

Born in Minneapolis, Minnesota, Willa Lou Pelini was working as a pastry chef in Washington, D.C., when fellow chef Paola Velez came to her with the idea for Bakers Against Racism. Willa was aiming for eighty people to join in their bake sale, but instead they sparked a global movement that ignited solidarity for racial justice on five continents.

Glossary

Activist A person who campaigns to bring about change.

Boycott A movement or action in which people refuse to buy a product or take part in an activity as a way of expressing strong disapproval.

Campaign A planned set of activities that people carry out in order to achieve something, such as political change.

Civil rights The rights that people have in a society to equal treatment and equal social opportunities, regardless of their race, religion, gender, sexual identity, disability, age, or other personal characteristics.

Democracy A government that is run by the people.

Demonstration A march or gathering that people take part in to show they are against something or they support for something.

Emancipation Proclamation The proclamation issued by President Abraham Lincoln on 1 January 1863, that enslaved people in Confederate states were 'forever free'.

Freedom Rider Someone who participated in the Freedom Rides, bus trips through the American South in 1961 to protest segregated seating in interstate buses and terminals.

Human rights The basic rights and freedoms that belong to every person.

Inequality Occurs when things are not equal.

Justice Fairness in the way that people are treated.

Plantation A large farm producing crops like cotton or sugar that historically depended on the labour of enslaved people.

Protest The act of saying or showing that you object to something.

Racism The harmful belief that one race is better than another and the behaviour driven by this belief.

Rebellion The act of not following the government's laws.

Segregation The division of groups of people by keeping them physically apart.

Sit-in A form of protest in which people occupy a space and refuse to leave until their demands are met.

Slavery When a person is treated as the property of another person.

Solidarity Showing unity within a group.

Underground Railroad A network of routes, places and supporters that helped enslaved people in the American South escape to the North.

Further Reading

The ABCs of Black History
by Rio Cortez and illustrated by Lauren Semmer

'Civil Rights Stories': *Racial Equality*
by Anita Ganeri and illustrated by Toby Newsome

'Civil Rights Stories': *Slavery*
by Catherine Chambers and illustrated by Toby Newsome

The Juneteenth Story: Celebrating the End of Slavery in the United States
by Alliah L. Agostini and illustrated by Sawyer Cloud

'Little People, Big Dreams': *Harriet Tubman*
by Maria Isabel Sánchez Vegara and illustrated by Pili Aguado

'Little People, Big Dreams': *Martin Luther King, Jr.*
by Maria Isabel Sánchez Vegara and illustrated by Mai Ly Degnan

Opal Lee and What It Means to Be Free: The True Story of the Grandmother of Juneteenth
by Alice Faye Duncan and illustrated by Keturah A. Bobo

Pies from Nowhere: How Georgia Gilmore Sustained the Montgomery Bus Boycott
by Dee Romito and illustrated by Laura Freeman

Timelines from Black History: Leaders, Legends, Legacies
by DK